WALSALL
PAST & PRESENT

BRITAIN IN OLD PHOTOGRAPHS

WALSALL
PAST & PRESENT

DAVID F. VODDEN

SUTTON PUBLISHING

Sutton Publishing Limited
Phoenix Mill · Thrupp · Stroud
Gloucestershire · GL5 2BU

First published 1999

Reprinted in 2003, 2004

Title page photograph: The former electricity power station, Reedswood, opened by the Mayor, Cllr T.P. Riley on 30 September 1949. This picture from the 1960s demonstrates well the emissions from this coal-burning generating station: it has now been demolished and the site given over to Sainsbury's, McDonald's and domestic housing. (Photograph courtesy of R.A. Brevitt)

British Library Cataloguing in Publication Data
A catalogue record for this book is available from the British Library.

ISBN 0-7509-2307-5

Typeset in 10.5/13.5 Photina.
Typesetting and origination by
Sutton Publishing Limited.
Printed in Great Britain by
J.H. Haynes & Co. Ltd, Sparkford.

To my wife, Elizabeth,
and our children, Richard, Catherine and Edward

THE BLACK COUNTRY SOCIETY

This voluntary society, affiliated to the Civic Trust, was founded in 1967 as a reaction to the trend of the late 1950s and early 1960s to amalgamate everything into large units and in the Midlands to sweep away the area's industrial heritage in the process.

The general aim of the Society is to create interest in the past, present and future of the Black Country, and early on it campaigned for the establishment of an industrial museum. In 1975 the Black Country Living Museum was started by Dudley Borough Council on 26 acres of totally derelict land adjoining the grounds of Dudley Castle. This has developed into an award-winning museum which attracts over 250,000 visitors annually.

It was announced in August 1998 that having secured a lottery grant of nearly £3 million, the Museum Board will be able to authorize the start of work on a £4.5 million state-of-the-art interpretation centre. This will be known as the 'Rolfe Street Project', named after the street which once housed the Smethwick Baths. The façade of this Victorian building is to be incorporated into the new interpretation centre.

At the Black Country Living Museum there is a boat dock fully equipped to restore narrowboats of wood and iron and different vessels can be seen on the dock throughout the year. From behind the Bottle and Glass Inn visitors can travel on a canal boat into Dudley Canal Tunnel, a memorable journey to see spectacular limestone caverns and the fascinating Castle Mill Basin.

There are 2,500 members of the Black Country Society and all receive the quarterly magazine *The Blackcountryman*, of which 124 issues have been published since its founding in 1967. In the whole collection there are some 1,800 authoritative articles on all aspects of the Black Country by historians, teachers, researchers, students, subject experts and ordinary folk with an extraordinary story to tell. The whole constitutes a unique resource about the area and is a mine of information for students and researchers who frequently refer to it. Many schools and libraries are subscribers. Three thousand copies of the magazine are printed each quarter. It is non-commercial, and contributors do not receive payment for their articles.

PO Box 71 · Kingswinford · West Midlands DY6 9YN

CONTENTS

Green Lane at the time of an experimental 12 mph speed limit, 1950s.

Green Lane with the Salvation Army Citadel, 1990s.

INTRODUCTION

This selection of pictures is a mixture of old views and current scenes, taken mainly by the author on the eve of the Millennium. As I wrote in my introduction to *Walsall Revisited*, 'during the twentieth century there has been a tendency to demolish the town centre and neighbouring buildings periodically and to re-build. In this way, many attractive, even medieval buildings have been lost and not all their replacements have met with widespread approval. Certainly, it was right to carry out slum clearance, but there were fine public buildings, private houses and commercial premises destroyed in the name of progress. . . .'

Several years ago, I was alerted by the late Percy Farmer to Sir John Betjeman's article of 24 August 1959 in the *Telegraph*, in which he described how he had spent a day of his holidays in Walsall, 'an ancient borough' which had

once been the centre of the leather trade . . . the streets were wide and comparatively free of traffic. There was a rich and splendid Town Hall, an impressive Victorian church by Pearson and then something quite unexpected and beautiful.

This was an old High Street with cobbled sides and trees: inns now turned into shops or offices climbing up to the Georgian Gothic west front of the parish church. This church was on a high, grass hill which had been cleared of stumps and laid out as a grassy space with a walled garden and a seemly row of two-storey modern flats in local brick designed by a good architect.

Walsall is a borough which is obviously proud of itself and I thought that if the local council were to turn this old High Street into something worthy of the charming and modest buildings, Georgian and Victorian, above the shop fronts it could be made into one of the most attractive streets in England.

Much of the redevelopment of Digbeth, Old Square and the High Street has taken place within a decade or so of Betjeman's visit and I have been fortunate in being lent pictures of the scene in the 1950s, as well as some showing the changes taking place in the 1960s, which I have matched with my own pictures of the present. Betjeman did not mention a most important ingredient which has made Walsall the community it is – the helpful and welcoming local people. I am particularly indebted to photographers Bob Brevitt, Don Payne and David Wilkins, among many others, all of whom I have acknowledged at the back of the book.

In addition to views of the changes in the town centre I have also included pictures of people and places from the edge of town, such as the Mellish Road Wesleyan Church. The Chuckery Cricket Ground, the Grange Farm, Brookhouse Farm and Park Hall are also pictured with their modern counterpart of housing and a school.

The changes, mainly of a generation or two, are startling when the old and new views are compared. Acceptance of these changes is always a matter of personal choice, but I think that the pictorial evidence will lead to one or two local legends being laid to rest, such as the Overstrand blocking the view of St Matthew's from Digbeth (see p. 36). Collecting the evidence has been most enjoyable and I hope it will provide hours of pleasure and interest for the reader.

This aerial view from the west, looking along Park Street and across the Bridge, to Digbeth, the High Street and St Matthew's, was probably taken in the 1940s.

CHAPTER ONE

BIRD'S EYE VIEWS

An aerial view of 1996, showing the town wharf development under way, although there is little evidence of the new art gallery by the canal basin. (Photograph courtesy of D. Wilkins, First House Photography)

The new art gallery from the air, July 1999. This view shows the entrance, with the large projection screen beside it which is designed to show pictures of the permanent Garman-Ryan Collection, as well as key items from temporary exhibitions. At the turn of the century, the Marsh Street area alongside is being considered for development as a 'Leather Quarter'. (Photograph courtesy of D. Wilkins, First House Photography)

This view from above Bradford Street towards the Bridge and Bridge Street, taken in July 1999, shows some of the new development of the Saddler's Centre, Tesco's and the edge of the new bus station alongside St Paul's Church. The well-established civic centre is at top left. (Photograph courtesy of D. Wilkins, First House Photography)

Seen from the Bridge towards Park Street is the Savoy Cinema (top left) and the roof of the railway station booking hall halfway down Park Street, 1955. The old bus station is in the centre and St Paul's Close is visible alongside the church. In the foreground is the George Hotel with adjacent Odeon cinema. Traffic is going across the Bridge and up and down Park Street. (Photograph courtesy of R.A. Brevitt)

Park Street and the new bus station seen from the air, 1999. This view shows many of the major redevelopments, such as the pedestrianisation of the town centre with new block paving in Park Street, leading up to the Woolworths store which replaced the cinema in 1997. The oval shape of the bus station is clearly shown, too. The market, established in the thirteenth century, continues to thrive. (Photograph courtesy of D. Wilkins, First House Photography)

St Matthew's from the air, with Bluecoat Infants' School still at the east end of the church, 1955. The school was eventually demolished in February 1963. The 'brotherhood' building (a church men's club) stood adjacent to the Memorial Gardens. It has been demolished and replaced by rooms at the parish hall. The Close was cleared and awaiting the building of the low-rise flats, visible in the next picture.

An aerial view of St Matthew's, c. 1979. It shows very clearly the church, its Close, parish hall, flats and the Memorial Gardens to the south-west. (Photograph courtesy of D. Wilkins, First House Photography)

St Paul's from the council house tower, 1953. The turret on top of the bus station of 1935 is visible, as is St Paul's Close. The skyline seems to boast more smokey factory chimneys than today. (Photograph courtesy of R.A. Brevitt)

A view of St Paul's from the tower, 1999. When this is compared with the previous picture a number of differences can be seen, such as the new art gallery and Town End office block with the new bus station under construction by St Paul's Church, which itself has a new turret on the roof. Distant chimneys do not seem so smoky.

The old fire station, Darwall Street, 1953. This was the headquarters for many years. The brigade was first founded in 1879, although a modest engine was kept in the porch at St Matthew's Church from the late eighteenth century. (Photograph courtesy of R.A. Brevitt)

The civic centre was opened in Darwall Street in 1976. This photograph was taken from the council house tower in 1999. The fire station has been demolished and replaced with new buildings in Blue Lane.

Lichfield Street from the council house tower, 1953. In the intervening years, several houses have been replaced by office accommodation and a large traffic island has been created by the Arboretum entrance. Here, Lichfield Street and Lichfield Road stretch away like an arrow. (Photograph courtesy of R.A. Brevitt)

Lichfield Street from the tower in 1999 shows how the trees have grown. In the middle distance, Norwich Union House and then the Health Authority office building are prominent.

The Black Swan and Neasham's from the council house tower, 1953. For a time the pub was known as The Stork and could be traced back to at least 1845. The name was changed to the Dirty Duck in the 1960s. It is situated in Leicester Square. (Photograph courtesy of R.A. Brevitt)

Leicester Square from the tower, 1999. There is not much change, but Neasham's has closed and the property is still vacant. The former Walsall Mutual Building Society office on the left which became the Heart of England Building Society continues now as a branch of the Cheltenham and Gloucester Building Society.

CHAPTER TWO

HIGH STREET,
OLD SQUARE & DIGBETH

This is an early view of the High Street, c. 1900. The trees are young and there is no evidence of petrol-driven vehicles. Halfway up the left-hand side stands the Guildhall, opened in the 1860s.

A local architect, Mr Gordon Foster, acquired the Guildhall when it had become derelict and restored it as a shopping precinct with office accommodation above.

Prince Charles meets and congratulates Gordon Foster, MBE, FRIBA, at the restored Guildhall, 1987. In the background is the then Vicar, the Revd Roger Sainsbury, who has since become the Bishop of Barking. (Photograph courtesy of G. Foster)

An earlier visit to Walsall by a Prince of Wales. HRH Edward Prince of Wales meets Queen Mary's Grammar School staff, 1923. During his visit he met ex-servicemen and also named Prince's Avenue after himself. (Photograph courtesy of QMGS Archive)

This view of High Street in 1958 shows how it was open to traffic during non-market days. Although the buildings on the bottom right are still there, Sainsbury's store has been built further up the hill replacing the People's Music Hall. (Photograph courtesy of R.A. Brevitt)

There is not a great deal of change between this picture of the High Street in 1965 and the last, except that it was taken from a little further down, next to the Woolpack, more or less where the Overstrand crosses today. (Photograph courtesy of D.J. Payne)

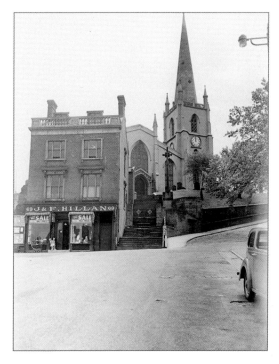

Looking up the High Street towards Church Hill can be seen Hillan's Draper's, the last shop, in 1955. In 1850 this site was occupied by a much less impressive shop, Rogers, a tea dealer.

Following a regular five-yearly inspection it was reported that the external stonework of St Matthew's Church needed extensive repair, so a restoration appeal was launched in 1980 for £410,000. The Vicar, Preb. John Jackson, was assisted by an appeal committee chaired by John Baker, JP. The work was eventually completed during the time of the Revd Roger Sainsbury, who recently became Bishop of Barking.

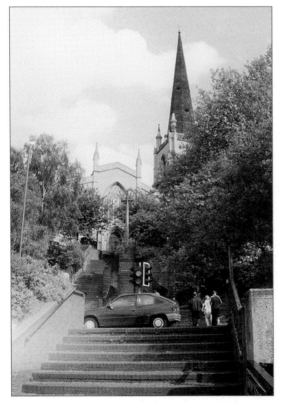

St Matthew's steps, 1999. After the pedestrianisation of the High Street, steps were inserted, leading to a pedestrian-operated crossing of Upper Rushall Street.

Mayor's Sunday parade for Mayor A. Stanley in 1936, led by Mr A. Felgate who is carrying a wand, as the Mayor's attendant. (Photograph courtesy of A.J. Felgate)

Civic Sunday for Mayor Cllr Keith Sears, 1995.

Upper Rushall Street and the Ditch redevelopment, 1950s. The men and bulldozers are clearing the sites of former houses and creating a slope for planting.

This view of St Matthew's from Upper Rushall Street clearly shows the success of the planting scheme, following the work shown in the previous picture.

Digbeth shops, north side, from just below the Woolpack, 16 April 1964. The Overstrand now bridges the scene at this point, but it was not possible in the old days to get a good view up the High Street to St Matthew's from here because of the bend in the street. (Photograph courtesy of R.A. Brevitt)

A scene from the Woolpack, looking down
the narrow street towards Old Square,
1965. (Photograph courtesy of D.J. Payne)

As can be seen here, the entrance to Old
Square in 1999 is now sealed by automatic
glass doors.

A view from the Old Square, 23 July 1963. It looks towards High Street past the rear of the Woolpack, allowing a glimpse of the former Clarendon Hotel, with its cupola, in Digbeth.

From the Old Square towards High Street, 1999. This scene provides quite a contrast with the one shown in the picture above. (By permission of Mrs A.A. Henderson, Old Square Centre Manager)

This is an artist's impression of how Old Square was likely to look in 1965. In the event, the bridge above was never built and the name 'Woolpack Passage' was not used.

Old Square redeveloped just prior to reopening is a more accurate record than the previous picture. Grey's became Debenham's. Since then, in 1987 the precinct has been roofed over and escalators installed. (Photograph courtesy of D. Wilkins, First House Photography)

Old Square looking towards the Leicester Square entrance, July 1963. On the left is Whitelegge's, jeweller's, and then the rear of the Palace cinema which was the first purpose-built cinema in Walsall in 1910. It is no longer possible to see the clock turret from this angle. (Photograph courtesy of R.A. Brevitt)

The view from Old Square looking towards Leicester Square and Freer Street, 1999. (By permission of Mrs A.A. Henderson, Old Square Centre Manager)

Looking from the Leicester Square end towards Old Square, 23 July 1963. This was taken from near the rear entrance to the *Walsall Observer* building. On the right, the steps led to the cinema, and next to the wool shop can be seen the rear entance to Harry Orton, the butcher's shop. In the centre, Davis the jeweller is next to Grey's, the china and picture shop. (Photograph courtesy of R.A. Brevitt)

The scene from the Leicester Square and Freer Street end, looking towards Old Square, 1999. (By permission of Mrs A.A. Henderson, Old Square Centre Manager)

Looking down Digbeth, 1965. Mock-Tudor fronts of the Woolpack and the Beehive are prominent. In the distance, the new development already includes Hawkins, who used to be near the Beehive. Now Hawkins is replaced by Mackay's. (Photograph courtesy of D.J. Payne)

Digbeth, from a similar viewpoint in 1999. The view is largely obscured by the Overstrand. The earlier variety of shop fronts has been replaced with a uniform redevelopment of reinforced concrete.

A view of shops in Digbeth on the south side, 16 April 1964. The shops begin on the left with Dipple, the butcher, then Collins' shoe shop, Shepherd's jeweller's, and then Parker's the greengrocer. (Photograph courtesy of R.A. Brevitt)

Digbeth shops on the south side, 1999. They now include the new Salvation Army shop, then the *Observer* and *Evening Mail* office.

The Old Still, demolished in 1959, looking east from the Bridge, 1930s. It had stood in Digbeth since at least the eighteenth century. It is said that Dr Johnson, who lived in Lichfield, caught the coach from here. (Photograph courtesy of Mrs N. Hilton)

Digbeth today, with new shops on the site of the former Old Still, and Dances' Tea Rooms where many residents enjoyed a leisurely cup of tea.

Demolition of Talbot Hotel taking place on 21 March 1963. It had been named after an extinct breed of hunting dogs associated with the Talbot family who became the Earls of Shrewsbury. The Mayor was recorded as entertaining guests there in the seventeenth century. (Photograph courtesy of R.A. Brevitt)

The former Talbot Hotel, Digbeth, is now partly an amusement arcade. This picture was taken on a Sunday morning in 1999 when cars are permitted to park in the market area.

The High Street, as seen from the Talbot, Digbeth, 1965. Already, the first stage of redevelopment had taken place. Although one can see the left-hand side of the High Street from here and Phillips' fish shop on the right-hand side in Digbeth, St Matthew's Church is out of sight. (Photograph courtesy of D.J. Payne)

High Street and Digbeth from the former Talbot, 1999. The photograph was taken through the same archway as the previous picture: this was an early part of the redevelopment of Digbeth. Nowadays the market stalls are left up all the time as there are four market days a week.

CHAPTER THREE

ST MATTHEW'S &
CHURCH HILL

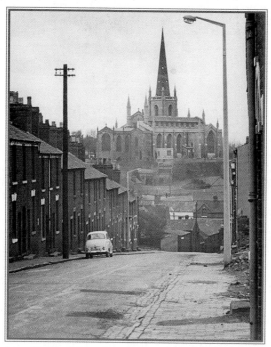

St Matthew's Church from Paddock Lane, c. 1960. This scene is much altered because so many of the terraced houses have been demolished and the high-rise Paddock flats were built on the upper part of the site. Paddock Lane probably got its name because it led to stables and pasture where horses were kept in coaching days. (Photograph courtesy of D.J. Payne)

St Matthew's Church from Paddock Lane. In the middle distance can be seen sheds and the gabled façades of Ablewell Street, which remain largely unaltered in 1999.

St Matthew's Church from Tantarra Street, *c.* 1960. Although terraced houses have been demolished, the school remains and has been converted to housing for the elderly by Walsall & District Housing Trust. Tantarra is thought to relate to the huntsmen's 'tally-ho' as they set off for the open countryside. (Photograph courtesy of D.J. Payne)

St Matthew's Church, from Tantarra Street, 1999. As with Paddock Lane, there has been demolition of housing, but the view from the middle distance to the parish church is relatively unchanged.

The Paddock from Church Hill, with a densely packed mixture of housing and factories or workshops, 1963. (Photograph courtesy of D.J. Payne)

The Paddock from Church Hill is much altered in 1999. The skyline is dominated by flats constructed in the 1960s, and much housing lower down the hill has gone.

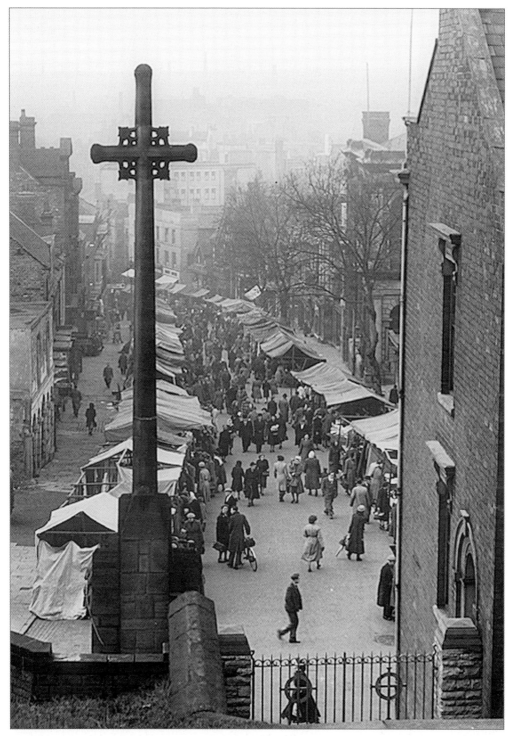

High Street and the market from the church, 1951. The picture is framed by the cross of the 1922 outdoor pulpit on the left and Hillans' Draper's shop on the right. The Guildhall on the right of the High Street was used as a court until 1976. (Photograph courtesy of R.A. Brevitt)

The same view of High Street and the market from the church in 1965 appears very similar. There seems to be quite a lot of atmospheric pollution in the distance, though. (Photograph courtesy of D.J. Payne)

Although in 1999 the cross on the left can still be seen, Hillan's shop has been demolished and the site landscaped. The Guildhall has been restored as a base for a number of retail outlets, and on the opposite side of the High Street there is now Sainsbury's store. In the distance can be discerned the new art gallery nearing completion at Town End.

Looking down Church Hill, *c.* 1900. On the left is a series of good Victorian houses with the Shakespeare Inn down on the corner. (Photograph courtesy of J.S. Hunt)

Looking down Church Hill, 1999. The houses have been demolished and the slopes landscaped. A few remaining doorsteps can still be spotted by looking through the railings near the bottom of the hill.

Above: This view of about 1900, looking up Church Hill, leads to the 'Brotherhood' building opposite the south porch of the church. (Photograph courtesy of J.S. Hunt)

Left: Looking up Church Hill at the end of the twentieth century, the eye is led to the Memorial Garden building which was designed to house the Book of Remembrance.

The Shakespeare Inn stood at the foot of Church Hill. It was a Georgian building with more ancient cellars from which it used to be possible to gain access to limestone mine tunnels. It was de-licensed in 1889 and became a lodging house. (Photograph courtesy of J.S. Hunt)

The site of the former Shakespeare Inn. This was demolished when the hillside was landscaped in the 1950s but the stone setts remain as a pedestrianised street.

The spire of St Matthew's Church being rebuilt in 1948. This picture was taken by the churchwarden, Mr Blanchard, who took many photographs during the restoration. (Photograph courtesy of Miss F. Blanchard)

St Matthew's spire, 1999. Steeplejacks have recently been up to repair the lightning conductor and to close the windholes with netting to prevent birds from nesting inside. The small devil sitting crosslegged above the clock is a replacement carved by Gordon Hericx in 1951.

Rebuilding the organ was also undertaken in 1952, during the incumbency of Canon Jenkins. This view is taken from the north gallery. At the rededication service, the hymn 'Ye Holy Angels Bright' was played to the tune Darwall's 148th, written by an eighteenth-century vicar of St Matthews. (Photograph courtesy of R.A. Brevitt)

Repairing St Matthew's organ, 1999. Here further work on the organ is being carried out by Nicholsons of Malvern. Parts of this very fine instrument date back to 1773 when Samuel Green built it. He was also responsible for the cathedral organs at Canterbury, Wells, Salisbury, Rochester and Lichfield.

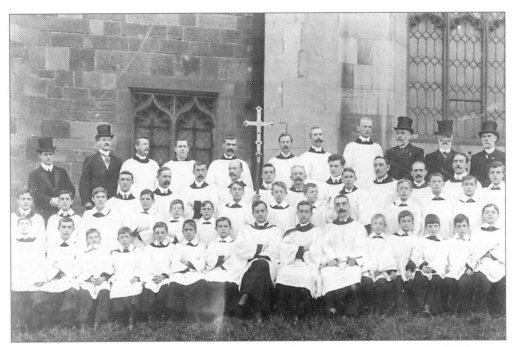

St Matthew's choir, *c.* 1906. The men in top hats, from left to right, are F.J. Cotterell, W. Wistance, D. Watts and H.A. Lynex (churchwardens) and Clerk G. Wincer. The Vicar is the Revd Arthur Paice (1901–18). On his right is the organist, G.C.E. Eyers, ARCM.

St Matthew's Church choir. This picture was taken by the author in 1993 to mark the retirement of long-serving verger Bill Millard, who is now a Chelsea Pensioner. Middle row seated, left to right: Revd M. Metcalfe, Mrs Beryl Metcalfe, M. Glazzard, Rector Revd Preb. M. Saunders, W. Millard, D. Stokes-Harrison, K. Masters, Revd P. Howell-Jones.

Princess Margaret at the Memorial Gardens, 1 May 1951, where she unveiled the memorial stone which is in the foreground covered by a Union Jack. The Mayor, W.R. Wheway, is at the microphone. (Photograph courtesy of Mrs P. Winton)

A view of the Memorial Gardens in 1999, after their recent refurbishing with the memorial stone carved by Gordon Hericx in the foreground.

This memorial stone in the Memorial Gardens was unveiled and dedicated by HRH Princess Margaret on 1 May 1951. The slate stone was carved by Gordon Hericx, lecturer in sculpture at Walsall Art College in Goodall Street.

A service was held in the Memorial Gardens to mark the fiftieth anniversary of D-Day on 6 June 1994. The Rector, the Revd Michael Sanders, was assisted by the Revd John Davies, Vicar of St Paul's, in the presence of the Mayor Cllr Keith Sears, Deputy Mayor Cllr Colin Beilby, Chief Executive David Windrush and members of the Normandy Veterans' Association.

CHAPTER FOUR

Upper & Lower Rushall Street, Goodall Street & Freer Street

*This view of Warewell Street flats was taken in about 1960, soon after they were completed.
The lack of traffic on a weekday is in sharp contrast to the scene today in the next picture.
(Photograph courtesy of D.J. Payne)*

Warewell Street flats, 1999. Because of the traffic it was not possible to stand in the road to use the same viewpoint as in the 1960s, as shown on p. 51.

St Matthew's from Lower Rushall Street as depicted by Vincent Murray in 1947. Although the site for the Warewell flats on the left seems to be derelict, the Borough Arms is shown on the corner of Upper Rushall Street. On the right, Eylands' Buckle works was still operating. Walsall Lithographic produced fifty prints of this drawing.

Lower Rushall Street today has car parking on the left. The Borough Arms stands isolated in Upper Rushall Street, the other shops having been demolished. On the right, Eylands' works has been restored as housing and one can still detect archways and other details from the previous picture.

Crabtree's original works in Upper Rushall Street, established in 1919. This building has now been converted to accommodation for the Lyndon House Hotel. (Photograph courtesy of A. Preston.

J.A. Crabtree, working at Upper Rushall Street. The founder of the firm was not only an inventor, but he also had good practical skills. (Photograph courtesy of A. Preston)

The former New Royal Exchange has been renamed the Lyndon House Hotel in the 1990s. Another pub, the Bull's Head, used to stand across the road.

Towards the end of the 1990s, this scene shows how Lyndon House Hotel, having replaced the New Royal Exchange, has taken over the building next door. Further expansion has taken place to the rear.

This shows Crabtree's Lincoln Works from the air, sometime in the late 1950s. Beacon Street runs along the main front and Prince's Avenue runs along the bottom of the site. At the upper left-hand corner, the former Chuckery Secondary School can be seen. Since ceasing recently to be the Tong Street site of the Art College it has suffered a serious fire. (By permission of D. Burwell)

Crabtree's 'Lincoln Works', established in 1926, is seen here partly demolished prior to the site being developed for housing.

David Wilson Homes being built on Crabtree's former site in 1999. It is planned to build over sixty, four or five bedroom detached houses here, at the end of Prince's Avenue. The development is to be known as Park View, as it overlooks the Arboretum.

The Masonic Hall in Goodall Street, 1964. (Photograph courtesy of R.A. Brevitt)

Tameway Tower in Goodall Street,
shown here in 1999, covers not
only the Masonic Hall site, but also
that of the gas office.

The Empire, Freer Street, 1954. Having been formerly a temperance hall, it became one of six town centre cinemas. (Photograph courtesy of R.A. Brevitt)

Freer Street. Debenhams now occupies the site of the Empire cinema. In the background can be seen the clock turret over the former Neasham's entrance to Old Square. This is part of R.G. Madeley's design from the 1930s.

Freer Street from the site prepared in Old Square for Grey's/Debenhams, 1960s. (Photograph courtesy of D.J. Payne)

Freer Street looking towards Bridge Street, 1999. This shows that, despite some demolition, the Black Swan still stands, as does the Wallpaper Warehouse.

Leicester Square, with the bunting displayed for the Silver Jubilee of George V, May 1935. (Photograph courtesy of Mrs N. Hobbs)

A new pedestrian crossing at the bottom of Freer Street in 1952, near the Black Swan, known in those days as The Stork. (Photograph courtesy of R.A. Brevitt)

CHAPTER FIVE

THE BRIDGE &
BRIDGE STREET

The Bridge and Clock. This was decorated in May 1935 for George V's Jubilee. The original clock, the 'four-faced liar', stands on the right and the buildings in the background include the Odeon cinema and the George Hotel. (Photograph courtesy of Mrs N. Hobbs)

A view of the Bridge, before the First World War, showing the original clock. The building on the right used to house the *Walsall Observer*.

The Bridge, looking north towards Lichfield Street, 1999.

The Odeon before refurbishment, showing *SW to Sonora* (distributed in the USA as *The Appalosa*), made in 1966 with Marlon Brando. (Photograph courtesy of D. Wilkins, First House Photography)

The Odeon refurbished, showing *The Jokers*, made in 1967 with Michael Crawford and Oliver Reed. (Photograph courtesy of D. Wilkins, First House Photography)

A view of the Odeon foyer, before refurbishment in the 1960s. (Photograph courtesy of D. Wilkins, First House Photography)

A view of the Odeon auditorium, before refurbishment. (Photograph courtesy of D. Wilkins, First House Photography)

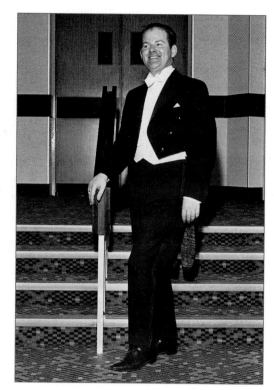

Phil Cross, manager of the Odeon for many years. (Photograph courtesy of D. Wilkins, First House Photography)

The Bridge, showing not only the bad weather conditions but also the style of road traffic of the time, winter 1951. Currently the Bridge is pedestrianised and the Sister Dora statue, originally in white marble, has been replaced by a bronze version since 1957. (Photograph courtesy of R.A. Brevitt)

A dramatic scene of the Bridge in a snow storm, 1952. (Photograph courtesy of R.A. Brevitt)

The Bridge, occupied permanently by 'The Hippo', 1999. Dunn & Co. have vacated the corner premises and the old clock has been replaced by a new one (out of shot to the left).

Bridge Street, and the Rayco van heads through the town centre, July 1977. Recently W.J. Ray have relocated to Leamore. (Photograph courtesy of T. Butler)

The Bridge on 28 June 1999 looks relatively free of traffic because it had been closed for the 'Freedom of the Borough' march by the Staffordshire Regiment. It is, in fact, closed to all but buses and taxis on weekdays. The modern clock can be seen on the Bridge and conversion work is under way at the former BHS building next to Lloyds TSB bank in the centre of the picture.

The 1935 bus station, seen here in 1954. Trolley buses were still used until 1970. (Photograph courtesy of R.A. Brevitt)

The new bus station under construction, 1999. In plan it will be oval and will contain offices, waiting-rooms and toilets, and will open early in 2000.

The Bluecoat School, 1934. This was demolished to make way for the bus station, which was built the following year. The school was re-established in Springhill Road. (Photograph courtesy of A.J. Felgate)

St Paul's Close, alongside the church, contained a row of fine town houses. They are seen here on 14 November 1953, but were demolished a few years later to be replaced by offices which included the careers service, FPA and a bank. The site has been cleared again to make way for the new bus station. (Photograph courtesy of R.A. Brevitt)

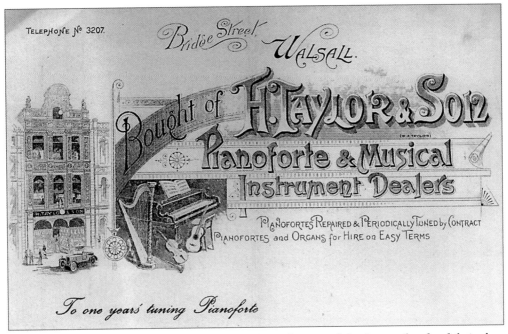

H. Taylor and Son's music shop billheading includes a drawing of the famous façade of their shop in Bridge Street. The premises have since been occupied by West Midland Travel and are now an HFC bank.

The Household Finance Corporation plc, trading as the HFC Bank. This was formerly Taylors' music shop and has retained the fine internal staircase of 1893.

This fine building is also in Bridge Street and now houses the Halifax. The new part on the right-hand corner has replaced premises which were once Elliott the chemists. (Photograph courtesy of C.D. Partridge)

The Halifax Building Society, seen here in 1999, occupies the building seen in the picture above, which has undergone some changes in detail. The corner is now the Halifax Property Services office.

The County Court House, shown in a pre-First World War picture, taken from a lantern slide. This building, costing 1,600 guineas, was intended for a library in 1836, then was renamed St Matthew's Hall. Eventually it became the county court. More recently it has become a restaurant, while court is now held in the former Co-operative building in Upper Bridge Street. (Photograph courtesy of D.J. Payne)

A view of the Old Court House, now a restaurant, with flower beds and pedestrian crossing in front, 1999.

CHAPTER SIX

DARWALL STREET, ST PAUL'S, LICHFIELD STREET & MELLISH ROAD

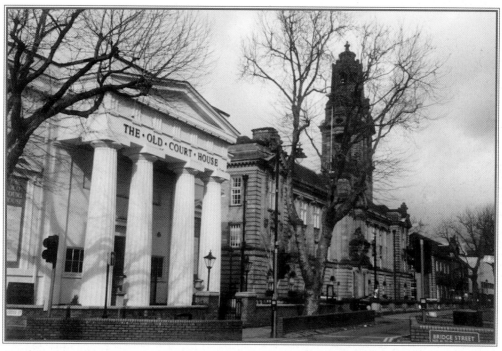

Another view of the Old Court House and Council House, 1999. The Council House, designed by J.S. Gibson FRIBA, was opened in 1905 when E.T. Holden was mayor.

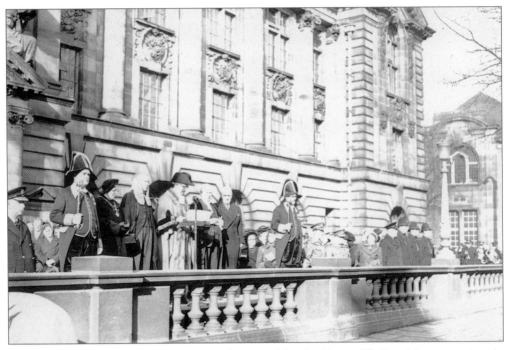

The proclamation of the Queen's accession being read by the Mayor, Cllr Tom Mayo, a partner in Fraser Wood & Mayo, estate agents, in front of the Council House, 1953. (Photograph courtesy of R.A. Brevitt)

The Mayor, Cllr Mrs Doreen Farrell, takes the salute as 1st Battalion Staffordshire Regiment, led by the Corps of Drums and the Clive Division Band, perform a 'Freedom of the Borough' march through the town with bayonets fixed, 28 June 1999.

Demolition of the old Tower Street baths in front of the fire station, in preparation for the construction of the present Gala baths, 1960. (Photograph courtesy of Mrs N. Hilton)

The Reedswood electricity power station cooling towers and the fire station in Darwall Street, seen from the council house tower in 1953. (Photograph courtesy of R.A. Brevitt)

Fire sub-station crew and equipment, Crabtree's, 1940–1. The car belonged to F.O. Bates, headmaster of Chuckery Junior School. It was used to tow the Coventry Climax pump. From left to right are: H. Lloyd, F.O. Bates, ? Crutchley, H. Benton, R. Ferriday, H. Hawkes, A. Jeffery and K. Jeffery. (Photograph courtesy of K. Jeffery)

Walsall fire brigade practising, probably to the rear of the fire station in Darwall Street, in 1951. (Photograph courtesy of R.A. Brevitt)

West Midlands Fire Service Blue Watch at Blue Lane Fire Station, 1999. Back row, left to right: John Grimshaw, Wayne Green, Stuart Tedstill, Ian Warden, Kevin Burns. Third row: John Callaway, Andrew Holman, Michael Bell. Second row: Roy Dobson, Andy Cooper. Front row: Station Officer John Kempson. (Photograph courtesy of E. Ockenden, WMFS)

St Paul's nave before re-ordering. This picture was taken on the Saturday morning when the organ was dismantled for sale to Shifnal. In the event, the organ was sold abroad without being rebuilt at Shifnal.

St Paul's new worship area. The glass screen looks into the well where the large glass crucifix is suspended.

Above: The Imperial cinema as a bingo hall, 1993. It had been built originally as an agricultural hall, and was then renamed St George's Hall. In 1881 it was converted to a theatre with almost 2,000 seats, but was converted to a cinema in 1908.

Right: The Imperial has now become a public house, as have other properties in Leicester Street, and in 1999 the exterior shows slight changes, not least the fine lamps.

Reginald Tildesley Ltd in Lichfield Street, late 1960s. Note the roadside petrol pump. Tildesley's later moved to Wolverhampton Street to become a main Ford dealer. (Photograph courtesy of Professor O. Naddermier)

Tildesley's former premises have now been taken over by Milligan's and an oyster bar. The façade has not been treated over-sympathetically.

W.T. Neal's office and adjoining building, late 1960s. The façade is of classical design and the porch and cornice of good proportion. (Photograph courtesy of Professor O. Naddermier)

The same building in 1999 is now occupied by MG Financial Services. The large ionic columns of the porch have been changed to a shallower porch with pilasters and the proportions altered radically by the insertion of a pediment. The replacement of the low front boundary wall by gentle steps is an improvement.

Wesleyan & General Insurance offices, late 1960s. Addison Cooper's pillared porch is two doors away. This is an attractive scene, showing the natural brick façades and windows with glazing bars. (Photograph courtesy of Professor O. Naddermier)

Addison, Cooper, Jessop & Co. remains relatively unaltered although the local authority has planted shady trees along the pavement. Some of the alterations in the former Wesleyan & General buiilding have been less sympathetic.

Lichfield Street, stretching from Addison Cooper's to Pritchard Cycles. This group of houses and offices has suffered some change in recent years, as shown in the picture below. (Photograph courtesy of Professor O. Naddermier)

Lichfield Street, from the Health Authority offices to those of Braden-Trubshaw, solicitors. On the left of the picture is the Health Authority and next to it is Crookes' office which was built originally by Jackson the builders as their head office. At that time there was a joinery shop to the rear, hence the initials in the gable.

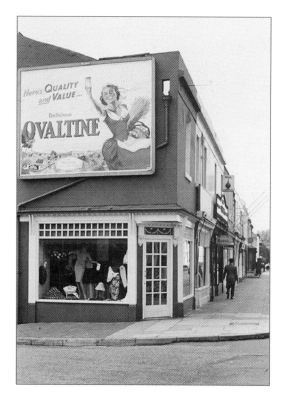

Dorothy Rowley's shop, adorned with an Ovaltine advertisement, late 1960s. Dorothy Rowley established her business there after working at Bodenhams in Upper Bridge Street. (Photograph courtesy of Professor O. Naddermier)

Rowley's shop is still a dress shop in 1999. The advertisements on the wall above show significant changes, including the Mayflower Chinese Restaurant which occupies the first floor of an adjoining property in Lichfield Street.

A circus parade, Broadway North, 1950. This parade was probably on its way to the Arboretum. (Photograph courtesy of R.A. Brevitt)

The same part of Broadway North, 1999. The elephants have gone, as well as the children. The tree in the front garden is now but a stump.

Above: St George's Church, at the junction of Persehouse Street and Walhouse Road. Designed by Robert Griffiths of Stafford in a geometrical style, it was built between 1873 and 1875. The intention was to add a tower and spire but these were never built, and it was demolished in 1964. (Photograph courtesy of K. Rock)

Left: St George's Church interior was highly decorated, and these solid pillars were made of York stone. (Photograph courtesy of K. Rock)

Walhouse Close, Persehouse Street, the site of the former St George's Church. The low walling is formed by the lower courses of the stone wall that formerly surrounded the church.

St George's Church choir, *c.* 1928. Back row, left to right: W Cheadle, -?-, -?-, -?-, ? Reynolds, Frank Hadley, -?-, -?-, -?-, -?-, Ernest Morgan, Frederick Fulton, Harry Plater (verger). Middle row: -?-, -?-, C. Badger, Frank Cookson, Bert Guest, the Revd Mr Renfrew, -?-, -?-, Sid Roper, Harry Wilkes, Lewis Hubble. Front row: -?-, Harry Ladbury, -?-, -?-, -?-, -?-, -?-, -?-, ? Doley, Ralph Dudley.

Frederick Augustus Fulton, a chorister in the previous picture, served in the RAMC in the First World War. He worked in the saddlery industry on his return. (Photograph courtesy of Miss A. Hunt)

Leonard Nock, aged fourteen, choirboy at St George's in 1932. He joined the choir after the group picture on p. 87. (Photograph courtesy of L.G. Nock)

Mellish Road Methodist Church, seen on a picture postcard in its heyday. (Photograph courtesy of Dr C. Hollingsworth)

Mellish Road Methodist Church, 1999. It is now a Grade II listed building and, although damaged by some subsidence, there are plans to restore it to be used as a homoeopathy centre.

The wedding of Terry Bingham and Julie Tolley at Mellish Road Methodist Church, 23 May 1981. (Photograph courtesy of Mrs N. Hilton)

Moss Close School, the long front, 11 February 1963. For some years this had housed the Queen Mary's Grammar School preparatory department and the first year of main school. When the new buildings were ready in Sutton Road this became redundant and was eventually demolished. (Photograph courtesy of R.A. Stone)

Moss Close. This was taken two years earlier, on 19 April 1961, when it was occupied by the grammar school. (Photograph courtesy of R.A. Brevitt)

Another scene of Moss Close School, showing the conservatory at the rear, 11 February 1963. (Photograph courtesy of R.A. Stone)

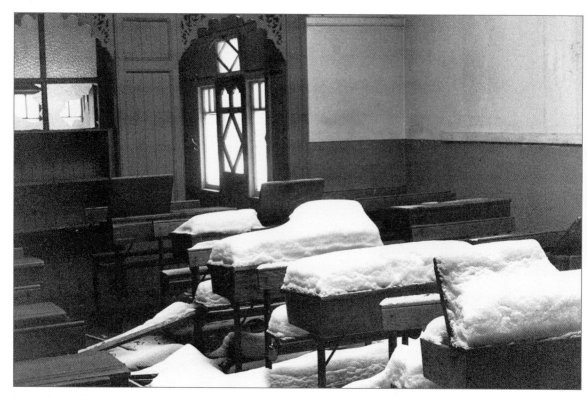

Moss Close School classroom with snow, 11 February 1963, during the very bad winter of 1962–3. (Photograph courtesy of R.A. Stone)

The houses of Moss Close on the site of the former school, 1999.

CHAPTER SEVEN

PARK STREET

Town's End Bank by J. Fullwood in the late nineteenth century. The triangular site was earmarked for a prestigious town hall, but this was abandoned in favour of Her Majesty's Theatre in 1900. The composition of the buildings in this picture makes them individual yet unified, being in the same materials and the same vernacular style. (Picture courtesy of G. Whiston)

Above: A picture postcard of the Savoy cinema, 1938. This was the first project for R.G. Madeley in 1936 when he joined the local practice which became Hickton, Madeley & Partners. The film, *The Joy of Living*, was made by RKO in 1938, starring Irene Dunn and Douglas Fairbanks Jnr. (Photograph courtesy of J.S. Webb)

Left: The cinema and its architect, R.G. Madeley FRIBA, in 1995, prior to demolition of the building.

At the top of Park Street, 1965. This picture suggests that some of the buildings were due for replacement by this time, and the Quasar Centre was built. (Photograph courtesy of D.J. Payne)

At the top of Park Street, part of the Town Wharf development, 1999. The new paving and street furniture, such as the street lamps, fits in well with the Quasar Centre.

HRH Princess Margaret at the station, 1 May 1951. The station clock stands at ten to two. Ahead of her the Princess had a busy schedule, dedicating the Memorial Gardens, presenting new Colours to the Sea Cadets and visiting W.R. Wheway's chain works. (Photograph courtesy of R.A. Brevitt)

The Park Street station entrance, seen here in 1999, is through the Saddlers Centre next to Marks & Spencer. The fine cast-iron entrance of the prestigious LMS station was dismantled in 1978, and is in storage.

Bill Pickering being driven down Park Street after his cross-Channel swim on his way to a civic reception, 1955. (Photograph courtesy of R.A. Brevitt)

While the Digbeth market area was repaved there was a temporary market in Park Street, and on the Bridge. This scene is from 10 May 1997.

The railway station from Town End House showing the cast-iron canopy of the LMS station and its large semi-circular booking hall, 1960s. (Photograph courtesy of D. Burwell)

Marks & Spencer now stands on the former station booking-hall site and the station is entered through the Saddlers Shopping Mall. The buildings to the right of the station have recently been replaced.

The former South Staffordshire Railway station entrance, Station Street, 1960s. The façade was designed by an ex-pupil of Queen Mary's Grammar School, Edward Adams, architect of Westminster. This was the main entrance from 1849 until a new entrance was built in Park Street in 1884. (Photograph courtesy of D. Burwell)

A view of the station entrance, Station Street, 1996. This had resulted from the late 1970s building of the Saddlers Shopping Centre. The left-hand side of Station Street has been restored with a new Superdrug store at the end as a result of the Town Wharf development.

Her Majesty's Theatre, when the area was decorated to celebrate George V's Silver Jubilee on 6 May 1935. (Photograph courtesy of Mrs N. Hobbs)

The new Woolworths under construction, 15 February 1996. This occupies the 'anchor site' of the Town Wharf development by Chartwell Land.

Park Street, showing a busy pedestrianised shopping area leading up to the newly built Woolworths site, 19 August 1996.

Park Street from the Bridge, May 1935. Lloyds Bank, now joined with the TSB, continues to occupy the right-hand corner but traffic is now excluded. (Photograph courtesy of Mrs N. Hobbs)

The Red Lion, preserved in the midst of the new buildings under construction, seen here on 15 February 1996. On the right is the steel frame for Woolworths on the site of the former cinema.

The Red Lion, safely flanked by new stores, in the completed new development including Ottakers bookshop and BHS, 1999.

CHAPTER EIGHT

BRADFORD STREET, WEDNESBURY ROAD & SOUTH WALSALL

The Bridge traffic in 1954 is in sharp contrast to the relatively traffic-free scene today. This is looking from the Midland Bank corner towards Digbeth where Buxton & Bonnet still straddles the entrance to the shopping arcade of 1900. (Photograph courtesy of R.A. Brevitt)

PC Peter McCracken directing traffic in Bradford Street, *c.* 1953. This is now pedestrianised as far as Bradford Place. (Photograph courtesy of D.P. McCracken)

Bradford Place, 1960s. This view was taken from the rooftop and shows the buses in the centre, with a refreshment vehicle for bus crews at the right-hand side. (Photograph courtesy of D.J. Payne)

Bradford Place, 28 June 1999. The refreshment vehicle has gone and so have the Midland Road railway sheds in the background.

Bradford Place, 1965. This shows the former range of shops, culminating in the jewellers on the corner of Park Street. Through-traffic is able to travel across the Bridge or up Park Street. (Photograph courtesy of D.J. Payne)

Bradford Place in 1999 boasts the Saddlers Centre on the left, along with a new range of shops, although those on the right-hand side are recognisable in the picture on p. 105. Traffic has gone, apart from buses and taxis.

Bradford Place from the racecourse, based on a drawing of 1840 which was tinted in 1913 by thirteen-year-old Master H. Stone, who was a pupil in the school being run in the porticoed building in the centre of the long block on the right. (Photograph courtesy of R.A. Stone)

To take a picture of Bradford Place from the racecourse is no longer possible. This is because supermarkets are all that can be seen from the site of the racecourse in 1999.

Today it is only possible to get a good view of Bradford Street from Midland Road on the far side of the supermarkets. The far right end of the block, just out of the picture, is Belsize House, the birthplace of Jerome K. Jerome, author, of – most famously – *Three Men in a Boat*, and journalist.

Just behind Belsize House at the junction of Lower Hall Lane with Caldmore Road, the end building in 1952 was Roebuck's General Store. The owners also used to sell ice-cream on the market. (Photograph courtesy of R.A. Brevitt)

Lower Hall Lane. The Roebuck General Stores shop has been replaced by an office block, which used to house the Social Services Department and has recently been renamed Millennium House.

The General (Sister Dora) Hospital, late nineteenth century. This was the inspiration of Sister Dora and was opened in 1878, the year she died, but she was too ill to attend the ceremony. It has now been demolished, apart from the former nurses' home which is divided into flats. The site has been developed by a partnership between Accord and Caldmore Housing Associations. An Edward VII pillar box still stands on the right-hand corner.

The demolition of the General Hospital, under way in 1997. It has been replaced with Housing Association dwellings. St Mary's the Mount Catholic church is in the background.

Housing Association dwellings, 1999.

During the coal strike in 1951, householders collected coal from the coal yard in Midland Road. (Photograph courtesy of R.A. Brevitt)

During a milk strike in 1951, housewives turned up at the former Co-op Dairy in Midland Road to collect supplies. The site is now occupied by a new probation centre. (Photograph courtesy of R.A. Brevitt)

The new probation centre, opened by the Queen in June 1994 on the site of the former Co-op Dairy. It contains interview rooms and workshops, and was designed by WMBC Property Service architects.

Zeppelin bomb damage at the front of the former Wednesbury Road Congregational Church, which was eventually demolished in 1973. (Photograph courtesy of Mrs M. Ward)

The Glebe Centre has replaced the Wednesbury Road Congregational Church, while the congregation has joined the Broadway United Reformed Church.

Tram no. 40 at the generating station in Darlaston Road, 1892. Despite being numbered 40, this was Walsall's first electric tram. On the left is open country. (Photograph courtesy of P. Abbott)

Whittalls Wines, Darlaston Road. In 1999 this occupies not only the former electric tramway generating building, but also the former Partridge steelworks – and there is no sign of open country

Children giving dance displays as part of the Coronation celebrations in 1953 on the Saddlers' former ground, Fellows Park. The site is now occupied by Morrisons supermarket. (Photograph courtesy of R.A. Brevitt)

Roy Whalley, Walsall Saddlers FC Secretary since 1984, at Bescot stadium which has replaced Fellows Park.

Walsall Saddlers FC, 1959. Back row, left to right: Colin Askey, Tim Rawlings, Stan Jones, John Christie, Peter Billingham, John Davies, Roy Faulkner. Front row: Albert McPherson, Tony Richards, Bill Guttridge, Ken Hodgkisson, Colin Taylor.

Walsall Saddlers FC enter the First Division, 1999. Back row, left to right, Richard Green, Chris Marsh, Andy Rammell, Michael Ricketts, Ian Roper, Matthew Gadsby, Tony Barnes. Middle row: Tom Bradley (physio), Mick Kearns (coach), Dion Scott, Darko Mavrak, Gabor Bukran, Jimmy Walker, Carl Emberson, Siggi Fyjolisson, Adrian Viveash, Bjarni Larusson, Bill Jones (youth development officer), Mick Halsall (youth team manager). Front row: John Keister, Mark Robins, Tony Daley, Neil Pointon, Paul Taylor (director of football), Ray Graydon (manager), Jason Brissett, Darren Wrack, Alfie Carter, Dean Keates. (Paul Kyte, *Walsall Advertiser*)

Sister Dora (Dorothy Pattison) pioneered Walsall's hospital 1865–78. Here is her statue wearing a Saddlers scarf, when the team was promoted to the First Division in 1999.

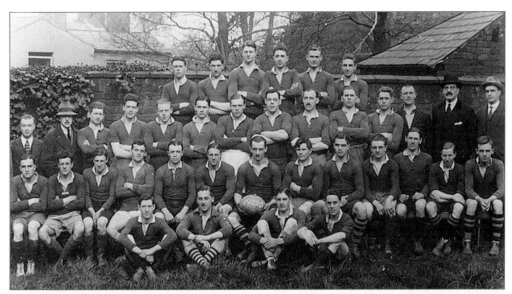

Walsall RFC Foundation Year, 1922–3. Back row, left to right: -?-, -?-, -?-, -?-, -?-, J.R. Bayley. Second row: -?-, A.J. Ralph, -?-, -?-, -?-, -?-, -?-, -?-, -?-, -?-, W.A. Burn, N. Franks, -?-, G. Wears, E.H. Green, -?-. Front row: -?-, -?-, -?-, -?-, -?-, E. Farmer, H.S. Holden, A.S. Arnewson, J.S. Bayley, -?-, -?-, -?-, -?-. Seated: -?-, A.R.J. Stanley, -?-, F.C. Seldon. The photograph was taken at the rear of the Wheatsheaf which served as their headquarters.

Walsall RFC, 1999. Back row, left to right: Harry Godsall (coach), Florencio Sequeira, Darren Robbins, James Baker, Richard Towe, David Godfrey, Richard Coleman, Rob Harding, Martin Jones, Mark Ellis. Middle row: Stacey McQueeney (chartered physio), Garry Green, Adam Smallwood, Barry Bodilly (chairman), Don Peacock (past president), Dr Kevin Connod, John Harper (selector), Geraint Tillott, Richard Henwood, Richard Marsh, Jim Deare (registrar). Front row: Matt Lane, Andy Walker, Nick Rose, Colin Jarvis (manager), Richard Mills (captain), David Rose (coach), Steve Lea, David Butler and Karl Jones. (Photograph courtesy of J.A. Harper)

Whitehall Junior School, champions of Walsall Schools, 1936–7. Back row, left to right: Cliff Withers, Stan Robinson, W.H. Middleton (head), Ken Proud, Bob Bennett, Graham Ward, P. Jowett (sports master), Ken Sharman, Leslie Gill. Front row: Ron Beech, Geoffrey Rock, Roy Groves, Tom Harris, Peter Howell. (Photograph courtesy of K.H. Proud)

In 1999 Whitehall School buildings are now occupied by the infants. The juniors moved to new premises adjacent to the University of Wolverhampton, the former site of West Midlands College of Higher Education, in the 1980s.

The new Queen Mary's Grammar School buildings in Sutton Road are seen here under construction in the 1960s. They were completed in 1965 and the school vacated the Littleton Street site, which was subsequently taken over completely by the Queen Mary's High School for Girls. (Photograph courtesy of QMGS Archive)

Queen Mary's Grammar School, 1999. The solitary boy entering the building is dressed for the heatwave on the first day of shirt-sleeve order. The school was founded in 1554 as a result of pressure from the local Hawes family.

The Elms in Sutton Road, 1953. At one time this was a private house, then Dr K. Anderson ran her surgery there. During the Second World War it was the Home Guard HQ and, in this picture, was being used by the TA. Harry Glaze's coach is from the firm he ran in Stafford Street. (Photograph courtesy of R.A. Brevitt)

Gordon House TA centre stands on the site of The Elms. In 1999 it is the base for the Royal Engineers.

Leila Williams in 1954 was the daughter of the landlord of the Wheatsheaf in Birmingham Street. She worked originally in a chemist's shop in Walsall, but later became a presenter with the BBC's *Blue Peter* programme. (Photograph courtesy of R.A. Brevitt)

In 1999 the Wheatsheaf has been renamed the Flock & Firkin. From its foundation Walsall RFC used it as its headquarters, and the picture on p. 117 was taken behind the Wheatsheaf.

Brookhouse farmhouse in 1952, just prior to demolition to make way for a private housing estate. (Photograph courtesy of R.A. Brevitt)

Elizabeth Road, leading to Gillity Avenue, runs across the site of the former Brookhouse farm, 1999. Brookhouse Road is named after the farm.

Park Hall, 1950. Seen here just before demolition, this was one of the last large houses to go. It was a little run down in 1939, but survived as an Officers' Mess for the duration of the war. It had been a fine house architecturally, and even the door furniture, which included silken panels, was of high quality. (Photograph courtesy of R.A. Brevitt)

Park Hall School now stands on the site of the Park Hall house. The avenue of trees lining Park Hall Road was planted when the house was built.

Grange farm, Sutton Road, 1953. The farm was owned by the local authority and farmed by tenants such as the Reece family, largely as a dairy farm. Mr Reece used to wear an old smock and deliver milk to householders. (Photograph courtesy of R.A. Brevitt)

141 Sutton Road now stands on the site of the former Grange farmhouse.

The cricket ground at the Chuckery, before it was replaced in 1909 by the ground at Gorway. In the middle distance stands The Shrubbery, the home of W.R. Wheway. Part of the ground is now occupied by a section of Prince's Avenue and by Willows Road. (Photograph courtesy of the late John Richardson)

The Shrubbery, the former home of W.R. Wheway, viewed from the junction of Prince's Avenue and Willows Road, 1990s. The windows remain unaltered, but the chimneys have been lowered. The house is now a training centre for the handicapped. Part of the original grounds is also occupied by the Fred Evans Home for the Elderly.

ACKNOWLEDGEMENTS

I would like to thank the following people for their help and encouragement and for the use of the old photographs in this book: Mr and Mrs B. Appleton, R.A. Brevitt, Mr and Mrs Bullock, D. Burwell, Miss S. Burwell, T. Butler, R. Champ, H. Cheadle, Mrs N. Clayton, N.E. Dunton, Mr and Mrs J. Dwyer, G. Evans, the *Express* and *Star*, T.D. Farrell, A.J. Felgate, B. Felgate, D.P.J. Fink, G. Foster, E. Fulton, S. Gill, J. Hamilton, J.A. Harper, Mrs A.A. Henderson, Manager of Old Square Centre, Mrs Norma Hilton, Mrs N. Hobbs, Dr C. Hollingsworth, G. Holloway, S.G. Holtam, Mr and Mrs Hough, Miss A. Hunt, K. Jeffrey, C.W. Lewis, D. McCracken, R.G. Madeley, R.J. Meller, Cllr E. Moorman, Prof. O. Naddermier, Mrs F. Neal, L.G. Nock, E. Ockenden (WM Fire Service), Mrs J. Parsonage, Mr and Mrs C.D. Partridge, D.J. Payne, Mr and Mrs E. Plater, A. Preston (Crabtrees), A.H. Price, K.H. Proud, L. Reynolds, late J. Richardson, K. Rock, the Misses Sankey, R.C. Shayler, R.A. Stone, Dr S. Taylor, *Walsall Advertiser*, Walsall Tec, Walsall Metropolitan Borough Council House Curators, *Walsall Observer*, Mrs M. Ward, J.S. Webb, G. Whiston, R. Wilcox, P. Wilkes, D. Wilkins (First House Photography).

Every effort has been made to contact owners of copyright of photographs where it did not rest with those who owned the prints.

BRITAIN IN OLD PHOTOGRAPHS

SUTTON'S PHOTOGRAPHIC HISTORY OF TRANSPORT